For Women Who:
Work Too Hard & Do Too Much
Learn To Delegate

Increase Professional Productivity and Reduce Stress

Carolena Lyons Lawrence, PhD

Published by
High Pointe Productivity

First Edition
ISBN: 978-0-9970768-2-0

Table of Contents

Acknowledgements

No woman is an island and no woman stands alone. The richness of this book is the value added from my support team. I have a team of great talent and great support.

I give humble gratitude to my editorial support team as follows:

Thank you *Mary Jackson Barlow* for your insight into what would be interesting to the audience, and for your time and wonderful suggestions to fine tune the book.

Thank you *Roz Head Lyons* for taking this journey with me and for sharing your talent of depth for details, reader insight, and process feedback.

Thank you *Dr. Patricia D'Souza* for your energy, intellectual stimulation, inspiration, and motivation to go back to what I know.

Thank you *Dr. Dorothy Blackwell* for your words of wisdom and your literary and linguistic expertise. Your words of encouragement have meant so much to me on this journey. Your market analysis has been right on point.

Thank you to my husband, *Otis J. Lawrence*, for the love, support, patience, and understanding in giving me the space to "do my thing", on this endless journey of intellectual stimulation and legacy.

Most of all, I thank my Lord and Savior Jesus Christ for all that I am and ever will be is by His grace, mercy, and love. "I can do all things through Christ who strengthens me".

Introduction

This book was born from a strategic leadership training seminar on delegation that I presented to ministers developing a strategic planning ministry.

During the seminar, many of the women participants provided me feedback that they were so pleased to receive such useful information that they were going to use it at their jobs. They indicated that they had never received that type of empowering training in the corporate arena but it was so much needed, especially for women.

After about a year or two after that seminar, while cleaning out my files, I came across my presentation notes from the delegation seminar and remembered the feedback from the women attending the seminar. I decided that the topic still had life that needed to be shared; therefore this book was borne.

This book focuses on delegation from a woman's perspective in the work environment. As women we tend to do too much, work too hard, work too long, and try to do everything ourselves, then we wonder why we are always so tried and stressed.

Women seem to have the need to make sure everything is done correct and feel that we are the only one that can get it done the right way. We too often feel the need to be busy and to be perfect. The problem is that perfect is a state of mind not a state of being. Things will never be perfect. The best we can do is get things in an acceptable comfort level for ourselves and then "let it go".

Where does that "need to be perfect" stem from? It probably comes from working in male dominated environments where we feel that we have to work even harder just to keep up and to show them that we are capable and should be there.

Please understand that the principles and strategies of delegation are standard and are not gender specific. Although this book is written specifically for women, the principles and strategies presented work in male dominated settings as well. There is no difference; men use the same principles.

An important principle that as women we should realize (which men already know), is that we need to master the art of delegation and try not to do everything ourselves. We must learn to delegate responsibilities to empower others. The more you empower others, the more powerful and successful you become. Bottom line, "we must learn to delegate effectively".

> *"You have to learn the rules of the game. And then you have to play better than anyone else."*
> *Albert Einstein*

We need to master delegation to set ourselves up for success by directing, training, and encouraging others. By not delegating, women can end up delaying decisions, which can cause problems for others.

> *"Things do not happen. Things are made to happen." John F. Kennedy*

Rather than attempting to do everything ourselves, we must assess who on our staff is capable of doing which jobs, has the knowledge, skills, talents, maturity, commitment, and experience to carry out various task. As a leader, our job is to nurture and develop the staff in their attributes to empower them to successfully take on tasks.

> *"Outstanding leaders go out of their way to boost the self-esteem of their personnel. If people believe in themselves, it's amazing what they can accomplish." Sam Walton*

Each chapter in this book presents elements to help you master the art of delegation. Keep in mind that this book is designed to empower you with knowledge and not to change you from your leadership style.

Throughout the book quotes are used for inspiration, motivation, and encouragement toward your success. The quotes are also there to make you think about how you can provide "valued added" quality to your work, and how to work smarter rather than harder.

"We may encounter many defeats but we must not be defeated." - Maya Angelou

An added bonus of delegation is that delegating can be used in all areas of your life. You can also delegate at home and in personal and social circles that you may be involved. Therefore, the art of delegation is not just limited to the work environment. You can practice the art in every part of your life.

Delegation will take time, work and will require us to overcome personal barriers to delegating; but it will be well worth it.

By delegating effectively, you will get your staff and others engaged in important and challenging work allowing them to develop their skills and to prepare them for their next level of responsibility. Most of all, delegating will allow you time to work on innovative projects and to take care of the bigger picture.

CHAPTER I

Set Up For Success - Delegate

Delegating is not new. However, for women delegation is an area that we don't have a great deal of experience; because the opportunities have mainly been in male dominated environments.

As I said in the Introduction section, the principles and strategies of delegation are standard and are not gender specific. They work the same in the male dominated settings. There is no difference; men use the same principles.

The focus for this book is for women because what we as women have to master is not trying to do all things ourselves. We have to learn to stay in our purpose and stay in our lane.

> *"Being the boss anywhere is lonely. Being a female boss in a world of mostly men is especially so."*
> *-Robert Frost*

We must keep in mind that other people are capable and we need to allow them to use their talents, skills, knowledge. Our job as business owners and managers is to take care of the big picture and let others take care of the small stuff.

Small stuff does not mean trivial or irrelevant, it just means it is not what is holding everything together. You are the leader, so lead your people to let their strengths make a difference in the solutions.

As women, we have to learn not to sit alone as the only judge. We must empower others to sit with us in carrying out decisions and tasks.

For business owners and managers, delegation is an essential skill, and is a leadership responsibility. The hazards of doing everything yourself can lead to burnout, stress and missed deadlines. You may get stretched too thin, or find that you don't have all the skills needed for the job. That's when it's time to delegate.

> *"Women need real moments of solitude and self-reflection to balance out how much of ourselves we give away."*
> - *Barbara deAngelis*

Besides streamlining your work and saving time, delegating teaches you to communicate persuasively, supervise and train, and expand your sphere of influence. Delegating includes building and maintaining a team.

"Coming together is a beginning; keeping together is progress; working together is success." - Henry Ford

There is more to effective delegation than mastering a set of skills and techniques. Delegating requires that you challenge your beliefs and your abilities, as well as those of others. In addition, you must demonstrate your confidence in other's ability to achieve success in the tasks you delegate to them.

> *"If everyone is moving forward together, then success takes care of itself."*
> - *Henry Ford*

This Chapter will help you to understand what delegation is in the work environment, and it will also help you to identify tools you can implement in the workplace to ensure that you delegate successfully.

Essential Skill

To delegate, you must give someone the responsibility and authority to do something that's normally part of your job or something that is new and has not been assigned. Delegation is the assignment of authority and responsibility to another person to carry out specific activities.

Delegation is not "dumping." If employees think you're merely throwing unpleasant assignments on their lap, they'll resent having to find extra time for boring or dead-end projects.

Delegation is not abdication. You share the accountability for the assignment. That's why you must establish appropriate controls and checkpoints to monitor your employees' progress (more will be discussed about controls in Chapter IV).

Delegation is sharing the responsibility, authority, and accountability with others and holding them accountable for their performance. Ultimately, as the business owner or manager, you hold the final responsibility.

> *"A leader is one who knows the way, goes the*
> *way and shows the way."*
> *- John C. Maxwell*

You must have a clear perspective and attitude about delegation, otherwise negative feeling and attitude will ripple to your team and send out the wrong message. Your team or staff will feel that you are just picking and dumping on them. Therefore, make sure you have a clear understanding of "What Delegation is NOT".

- **Delegation is not "dumping**." If employees think you're merely throwing unpleasant assignments on their lap, they'll resent having to find extra time for boring or dead-end projects.

- **Delegation is not "task assignment"**. Task assignment is assigning work to an individual with work duties and responsibilities. Delegation, however, is giving someone the responsibility, authority and accountability to an assigned task that would normally be part of the manager / owner/supervisor job.

  Let's be clear. If you do not give the person to whom you are assigning the task the full responsibility, accountability, and authority for the assignment, you have not delegated. Delegation is assigning tasks that are part of "your" normal job. That is why you must make sure you learn how to effectively delegate otherwise it will appear that you are just "dumping" your work on to someone else.

You will earn respect and creditability in the eyes of your team and staffs by letting them see that you have their best interest in mind and you want them to succeed. Keep in mind that your job is to direct, train and encourage. That is how you empower your team from the big picture.

"Example is leadership." - Albert Schweitzer

Elements of Delegation

Responsibility, authority, and accountability are the key elements of delegation. When you delegate, you share responsibility and authority with others and you hold them accountable for their performance. The ultimate accountability, however, still lies with you, the business owner or manager.

The three elements of delegation cover the concepts and practices of delegation. The elements are:

- Responsibility
- Authority
- Accountability

Responsibility

Responsibility in relationship to delegation refers to the assignment or project itself and the intended results. Responsibility means setting clear expectations. It also means that you should avoid prescribing the employee "How" the assignment should be completed.

We are always tempted to tell how one should do projects or assignments. However, at all cost, <u>do not tell "How"</u>. By telling "How", you take away the person's creativity, talent, and skills. You must avoid taking your creativity, talent, and skills and imposing it onto someone else.

When you delegate, you distribute responsibility and authority to others while holding them accountable for their performance.

Many small-business owners believe they can save time by telling their employees both what to do and how to do it. After all, in most cases you initially had to do all of the jobs now held by employees, so it makes sense to try to save them the effort of trying to figure things out for themselves ...<u>right</u>?

<u>Wrong</u>. Delegation is a better approach, because it launches employees into effective, independent action and saves time and resources in the long run. Each situation and assignment is unique, but here are three powerful steps that you can take to delegate more effectively:

> 1. Understand whether you are making a request or issuing a command. A request allows the person to say, 'No, thank you,' whereas a command there is no option. Don't leave yourself open for a "no, thank you" response if that is not what you want.

> 2. Make your request or command clear by including the following points:

> - The task you want done.
> - The reason it needs to be done.
> - When it needs to be done.
> - What resources (people, dollars, technology) you are making available for its completion.
> - What you expect the final product to look like.

- How you will make yourself available to answer any questions.
- An agreement on a midpoint check-in.

Faulty assumptions in any of these areas can result in problems and delays.

> 3. Don't skip your midpoint check-in. If, at that point, you find the person or team way off track, you may be tempted to micro- manage the remainder of the project or task. However, instead of micro-managing, reassess whether you made a clear request and whether your people are capable and motivated.

If you need to clarify the task again, do so. If your people are not capable or motivated, reassign the task to someone else. However, if no one else is available, assess the available talent and keep reassessing until they completely understand the task.

Delegating effectively helps you make the most of your resources, allows for greater overall productivity, and launches your employees into effective, independent action.

Authority

Delegation is the assignment of authority to another person to carry out specific job-related activities. Authority allows a subordinate to make decisions; it is a shift of decision-making authority from one organizational level to a lower one.

> *"Surround yourself with the best people you can find, delegate authority, and don't interfere as long as the policy you've decided upon is being carried out."*
> *-Ronald* Reagan

Authority refers to the appropriate power given to the individual or group including the right to act and make decisions.

> *"You can delegate authority, but you cannot delegate responsibility." - Byron Dorgan*

It is very important to communicate boundaries and criteria such as budgetary considerations and resource restrictions.

Sometimes, delegation is confused with participation. Difference is that in participative decision making, there is sharing of authority; with delegation, subordinates make decisions on one's own. For example:

As your business grows, you'll begin to accept the fact that you can't do it all — that your operation is too big and is growing too fast. You realize that you must pass along some of the responsibilities to others. You accept the fact that you must finally clear the "delegation hurdle," where you get over the barrier of: *"I'm a business owner who does everything"*.

Accountability

Accountability refers to having individuals answer for his/her actions and decisions along with receiving the rewards or penalties that accompany those actions or decisions.

> *"Accountability breeds response-ability."*
> *Stephen Covey*

Whether delegating is vertically or horizontally, delegation must be accompanied by effective direction, training, and encouragement. However, delegation will not be effective unless managers, owners, and supervisors work with employees to help them develop the skills needed to get the job done.

Delegation requires that you hold the person responsible for the effective execution of a task fully accountable for all aspects of the task. They must be able to explain their actions in the execution of the task and also explain the final result.

With effective delegation, accountability is required along with good communication and a high degree of trust between the delegator and the delegatee

Sometimes, however, under time pressures managers end up delegating without even knowing it. They're so busy that they may flag down the nearest employee and give only minimal instructions before moving on. That is not effective delegation because you cannot hold the person accountable without clear direction and training.

In any case, by treating delegation with more care, you can transfer responsibility and accountability to your team with a minimum of interruption.

> *"Be a yardstick of quality. Some people aren't used to an environment where excellence is expected." - Steve Jobs*

CHAPTER II

Why You Should Delegate

Even "Superwoman-You" need help and support. There is no shame in asking for assistance. Push aside the pride and show respect for the talent others can bring to the table.

And, remember that there is no such thing as a single-handed success: When you include and acknowledge all those in your corner, you propel yourself, your teammates and your supporters to greater heights.
*   - Author Unknown.*

Don't Hurt Yourself and Others

If you work on your own, there's only a limited amount that you can do, no matter how hard you work. You can only work so many hours in a day. There are only so many tasks you can complete during work hours. There are only so many people you can help by doing these tasks; because the number of people you can help is limited, your success is limited.

In addition, if you're good at your job, people will keep wanting even more from you.

With people wanting more and more from you, it can lead to a real sense of pressure and work burnout. You can't do everything that everyone wants, and this can leave you stressed, unhappy, and feeling that you're letting people down.

As women, we tend to do too much and expect just as much from others. One of the most common ways of overcoming the limitations of our time and energy is to learn how to delegate work to other people. If you do that well, you can quickly build a strong and successful team of people that are well able to meet the demands and challenges placed upon them.

All of that is why delegation is such an important skill, and is one that you have to learn.

> *"Don't be a bottleneck. If a matter is not a decision for the President or you, delegate it. Force responsibility down and out. Find problem areas, add structure and delegate. The pressure is to do the reverse. Resist it."* - *Donald Rumsfeld*

Avoid Trying To Do All and Be All

Besides streamlining your work and saving time, delegating teaches you to communicate persuasively, supervise and train, and expand your sphere of influence. It means building and maintaining a team.

You can help your staff stretch their talents, and grow through teamwork, new skills, and problem solving. Delegating gives more people a stake in the outcome which leads to more dedication and personal ownership to the task.

> *"The way you delegate is that first you have to hire people that you really have confidence in. You won't truly let those people feel a sense of autonomy if you don't have confidence in them." – Robert Pozen*

Delegation is more than hiring and managing people---it is guiding, inspiring, and motivating them. As women, guiding, inspiring, and motivating is what we do naturally with our family, now we just take that same talent to the work place.

Below are four steps to do a great job and not just a good job at delegating:

1. Free yourself to run your business and see the big picture.
2. Develop your employees and make them more valuable.
3. Spread accountability to encourage a stronger, more resilient team.
4. Respond faster to changes in your business when you can rely on capable employees to take charge.

Delegation is important because as business owners, managers, and supervisors we can't possibly be everywhere and doing everything all of the time. Many supervisors fear delegation because of the old adage, "If you want something done right, you have to do it yourself." _Get over it_ "superwoman" and reduce your stress.

When you get over it, you will find that effective use of delegation will motivate your staff while increasing their self-confidence, and providing them with opportunities to learn and grow through new experiences. This process will also allow you to assess the abilities of your staff while developing and training them at the same time.

Now we have a _win-win_ situation for everyone. Oh 'how sweet it is;' all because you delegated.

> _"I trust the people who are working with me. I delegate." – Mario Draghi_

As women, we tend to hold on tight, afraid to let go of tasks. "_Let go_, stay in your lane and purpose." Delegate and reap the benefits of multiply effectiveness.

Multiplies Effectiveness

Delegation done right offers multiple areas of effectiveness. The effective use of delegation can enhance the following:

- Motivate your staff while increasing their self-confidence,
- Provide them with opportunities to learn and grow through new experiences,
- Allow you to assess the abilities of your staff while developing and training them at the same time.
- Allow you to use your time and talents where they can make the biggest difference.

> *"I am learning how to delegate and how to empower people." – Tyra Banks*

In the following sections, more multiple effective delegation is presented. The more you know about the effectiveness of delegation, the better your opportunity to use it successfully. The key multiplier delegation effectiveness areas are:
- Reduce stress
- Emphasis on teamwork
- Train to replace up
- Benefit to managers/supervisors
- Benefit to employees
- Benefit to organization

Reduce stress

One of the most crucial and challenging tasks many women leaders frequently complain about is that they have too much to do and too little time. Unchecked, this feeling leads to stress and ineffectiveness. In many cases, women executives could greatly reduce their stress by practicing effective delegation.

> *"So I delegate a lot and I make my family come first, my husband and our kids." –Kelly Preston*

Successful businesses, regardless of size, encourage not only their managers and supervisors but also others to master the art of delegation.

> *"When you delegate work to the members of the team, your job is to clearly frame success and describe the objectives." – Steven Sinofsky*

Historically, delegation has been a vertical process, with managers and supervisors delegating to subordinates in a clearly defined hierarchical structure. However, today's successful businesses are emphasizing both horizontal and vertical delegation. The horizontal delegation is considered to be collaboration.

With horizontal delegation (collaboration), managers and supervisors are delegating lateral to other managers on the same hierarchical level. Delegation on both horizontal and vertical levels can lead to more cohesive and strong team structures.

"I think one of my strengths is that I can always take advice, and I can delegate. I know a lot of people feel the need to do everything themselves, but I am not one of them." - Dasha Zhukova

Emphasis on Teamwork

With more emphasis on teamwork these days, the ability to influence and delegate to others over whom you have no direct control is critical to the team's success.

What I mean by that is with horizontal collaboration you have no direct control over other managers and supervisors because they are not your subordinates. Therefore, you must establish a very good working relationship with your cohorts to have them be stakeholders in the tasks and willing to accept what you delegate to them.

Many support group leaders complain that they have to do everything themselves. They say that it's just too difficult to find others to whom they can delegate part of the load and rely on to perform well.

Part of the problem these leaders complain about appears to be caused by poor delegating skills.

"I'm going from doing all of the work to have to delegate the work – which is almost harder for me than doing the work myself. I'm a lousy delegator, but I'm learning." - Alton Brown

Simply put, the objective of delegation is not only to get the job done by someone else, but also to develop competent team members. The best of all things is that team members will eventually know everything the leader knows and will be able to share or take over the leadership role when necessary.

Delegating the simple tasks of following instructions and completing assigned work won't do the trick. Through effective delegating, leaders teach team members to:

- accept responsibility,
- think and make decisions,
- assure that desired results are attained independently of the delegator. [1]

To avoid lack of participation from team members, know your people's interests and capabilities. Never delegate tasks to them that they have no interest or qualifications to perform the task well.

As a leader, you must assess staff. If you don't understand your people's strengths, weaknesses, skills, and ambitions you will not be able to make effective matches between jobs and people. Mismatches invite failure, and no one benefits from failure.

---

[1] Mooney, Dick, (2015)

"In order to succeed, we must first believe that we can." -Nikos Kazantzakis

Train to Replace Up

 Do not miss opportunities to train your staff by assuming they have too much work to do and not delegate to them. That is a big mistake!

You should not be the person that decides what another person is capable of accomplishing. Your goal should be to train them to replace you. Delegation is grooming them to take over some of your duties to free you to work on the big picture, which means your must train them to do so.

Here are some common reasons why supervisors avoid delegating in the workplace. See if you recognize yourself in any of these reasons:
- Believe employees are too inexperienced.
- Believe it takes more time to explain how to do it than to do it yourself.
- Think if employees make mistake, "It's my fault."
- Believe employees are too busy doing other things.
- Worry people will think you are lazy or shirking your responsibilities.
- Think the task is different. It requires your personal attention.

- Think you have to approve the final product anyway, so might as well do it yourself.
- Believe that no one else can do it as well as you can.

It can be difficult to let go of familiar activities. In many cases, you might be able to do a better job than others. However, by failing to delegate, you can stymie the growth of employees and your own growth as a supervisor.

> *"What you do today can improve all your tomorrows."* - Ralph Marston

Advantages

Delegation Advantages to Managers

Major reasons why women managers and supervisors should master the art of delegating are:
- Avoid leading an army of one
- Move from doing to directing
- Promote professional growth and development of your staff
- Avoid the temptation of doing everything yourself
- Build promotable employees
- Get the best return on your personnel investment
- Make your job easy and exciting
- Reduces stress

- Make you look good
- Frees you to do what you should be doing
- Develop trust and rapport with your employees
- Groom your successor so you can move on to bigger and better things.
- Avoid derailing your own advancement by not having someone to take your place

"Infuse your life with action. Don't wait for it to happen. Make it happen. Make your own future. Make your own hope. Make your own love. And whatever your beliefs honor your creator, not by passively waiting for grace to come down from upon high, but by doing what you can to make grace happen… yourself, right now, right down here on Earth." -Bradley Whitford

Delegation Advantages to the Employee

The effective use of delegation will motivate your staff while increasing their self-confidence, and provide them with opportunities to learn and grow through new experiences.

"A creative person is motivated by the desire to achieve, not by the desire to beat others." - Ayn Rand

Delegation will also allow you to assess the abilities of your staff while developing and training them at the same time.

The following are some of the employee advantages from effective delegation:

- Provides professional growth opportunities
- Develops professional knowledge and skills
- Elevates self-image and ultimately self-esteem
- Enhances confidence and value to the organization
- Brings personal satisfaction and a sense of achievement
- Creates opportunities to be involved with decision making which in turn leads to more commitment and increased morale

> *"Believe in yourself! Have faith in your abilities! Without a humble but reasonable confidence in your own powers you cannot be successful or happy."* - Norman Vincent Peale

Delegation Advantages for the organization

Effective delegation can be a win, win, win for all. Delegation allows managers/supervisors, employees, and the organization to win. The following are some of the delegation advantages to the organization:

- Saves money by having more job satisfaction and increased morale among the staff, which leads to higher productivity and reduced time off from work
- Promotes teamwork by having the staff see

and understand the benefits of a team pulling together for the common and personal good
• Brings about professionalism by having well established standards that everyone understands and benefits from on an equal basis
• Increases productivity and efficiency by having the staff feeling that they are recognized for their value added to the company.

"With the new day comes new strength and new thoughts." - Eleanor Roosevelt

CHAPTER III

When to Delegate and to Whom

GRABBING THE GLORY — *Some high-ego leaders hog the credit for a person's hard work. Make sure you give the appropriate recognition to those who deserve it. If you must salute yourself, mentally pat yourself on the back for being a great delegator.*
Author Unknown

To figure out how to delegate properly, it's important to understand why people avoid delegating. People don't delegate because it takes a lot of up-front effort. Also, if you are a person with control issues, delegating will be a very big struggle for you, but you must persevere. To be more efficient, you will have to learn to give up control.

Giving up control by delegating does not come easy, it takes time to master. However, once you master the skill, you will be able to reduce the workload and provide opportunities for growth and challenge for the team, which can lead more job satisfaction.

> *"Optimism is the faith that leads to achievement. Nothing can be done without hope and confidence."* - Helen Keller

Support and Empower

As women, we usually find it easier to do the cerebral task ourselves rather than delegating to members of our team. We often believe it will take too much precious time trying to teach and show someone else how to do the task. We believe it would be much easier, more efficient, and faster to do the task ourselves. Well, it is time to rethink that belief.

You have probably heard, said, or thought about the saying "If you want something done right, do it yourself". While on the surface it's easier to do the task yourself than to explain the strategy of the project to someone else; however, there are other considerations to be made. Consider the following reasons why it is better to delegate the task to someone else:

1) If you have the opportunity to spearhead a cutting edge project, the chances are your skills are better used there in developing the strategy and coming up with ideas.
2) By doing the work yourself, you fail to make the best use of your time and also fail to support and empower yourself and others.
3) By meaningfully involving other people in the project, you support them by helping to develop their skills and abilities.
4) Because you have supported and empowered others, the next time a similar

project comes along, you can delegate the task with a confidence that it will be done well, with little or no involvement from you.

5) Delegation allows you to make the best use of your time and skills.

6) You are able to empower others by giving them the opportunity to grow and develop their full potential in the organization.

Best Match For The Task

The very first step in delegating the task is to identify what should and should not be delegated. The next step is to find the right person to delegate to by matching skills and personality to the task at hand. As a preliminary step in deciding on the best fit for assigning the task, ask each of your employees the following questions:

1. What would you like to learn more about at this company?
2. What areas would you like to expand your skills?
3. What parts of this company do you feel you know the most/least about?
4. Are you eager to change your current job duties in any way? If so, how?

Armed with the answers, you can delegate duties to people who are a match and receptive to accepting them.

Also consider the work habits of individuals on your team. Some people may need lots of explanation, while others only want to know your expectations and any guidelines before they are left alone to get the task done.

Assess your employees' strengths and make good use of their unique attributes to the task. Some tasks will not be cut-and-dry as to who receives which tasks.

If you are not sure who to assign tasks, make it democratic and present the task(s) to the entire team and discuss who is the best fit to effectively handle the task(s).

When you have a discussion with the team, be sure to be prepared with clarification of all goals, timelines, and objectives for the task. You want to avoid miscommunication.

Put the information in writing in an appropriate format that is easy to follow. Also include expectations and answers to possible questions your team may have.

To select the best person to delegate a task, listen and observe. Learn the traits, values, and characteristics of those who will perform well on specific tasks. Give tasks to people who will deliver and not to people who are the least busy.

Also, trust those you delegate tasks and give them the opportunity to do tasks their way.

> *"You're only as good as the people you hire."* - *Ray Kroc*

Surround yourself with reliable, confident, capable, and talented people; which in turn you will never have to worry about things being done right. However, keep in mind that it will take time, and work to find and hire those reliable and confident people.

> *"Leadership consists of picking good men and helping them do their best."*
> *Chester W. Nimitz*

Another important factor is that when you delegate, totally delegate the responsibility of problem solving. Avoid having your subordinates turning to you to solve every problem they face in carrying out tasks. Ask the subordinate to recommend solutions for problem they may bring to you. Get them to use their creativity to problem solve.

> *"Accept the challenges so that you can feel the exhilaration of victory."* - *George S. Patton*

Delegating gives more people a stake in the outcome and in the organization as well as giving them confidence and pride.

Authority and Respect

Authority and respect are important in dealing with your staff. Present yourself as a respectable authority on the job. Share with your staff that you respect and appreciate their willingness to be a team player.

After you have decided whom to delegate tasks, follow up with them on how they are coming along with their perception of the tasks. You want to make sure that they thoroughly understand the expectations, timeline, quality and are comfortable with the execution. In addition, follow up with assessment of progress, which is discussed in Chapter IV.

As I mentioned earlier, a fundamental principle in delegating is to also assign responsibility and authority; because power without accountability leads to abuse of power and loss of respect.

In addition, accountability without power is demoralizing. Team members should always be held accountable for the task(s) that has been delegated to them.

"Leadership is influence." –John Maxwell

Communicate with Everyone Involved

In delegating, be sure to inform all that will be affected by the delegation. When delegation involves granting rights to allocate and consume additional resources, out of respect, other parties need to know that you have delegated authority to a team member. Everyone affected by a project must be informed on what has been delegated.

Team members also need to know what resources are available to accomplish the tasks that are delegated to them and the level of initiative that is expected.

> *"Communication leads to community, that is, to understanding, intimacy and mutual valuing." - Rollo May*

Know When to Delegate

When done appropriately, delegation is a 'win-win' event. However, that does not mean that you can delegate just anything. To determine when delegation is most appropriate here are five questions you should ask yourself:

1. Is there someone else who has or can learn the necessary information or expertise to complete the job?

2. Is this a task that someone else can do or is it critical that you do it yourself?

3. Does the job give an opportunity for growth in developing someone else's skills?

4. Is it a job that will recur in the future?

5. Do you have enough time to train, answer questions, and monitor progress that is required for jobs delegated?

If you can answer "yes" to at least three of the questions, then it could be worth delegating this job.

Listed below is a guide to what to delegate and what not to delegate:

Delegate:
- day-to-day minor decisions
- minor staffing duties, such as scheduling, shift change etc
- routine duties that are expected when you are not there.
- tasks that can develop employees for potential promotion
- answer routine questions
- day-to-day clerical duties such as filing, sorting, routine reports

Do not delegate:

- morale issues
- off-job problems
- duties no one is qualified to do
- disciplinary issue such as probation or firing
- personally assigned task from your superior
- emergency or short-term task
- jobs critical to long-term success such as recruiting

CHAPTER IV

Know The Delegation Process

How do you get people to share the work and take on extra projects? How do you get people to share your vision and goals? How do you delegate?

One answer to those questions is to delegate right the first time. Well delegating the first time must be right otherwise you could lose credibility and respect.

Sometimes delegation can lead to undesired results or poor quality work. Therefore, delegate right the first time by thoroughly planning and communicating the delegated task.

> *"The first rule of management is delegation. Don't try and do everything yourself because you can't." – Anthea Turner*

Rebecca Morgan, 2015 shares the following tips for delegating effectively:

'But I gave you Instructions!'[2]

Have you ever delegated a task only to have it returned to you looking very different from what you had in mind?

What I have learned, regretfully, is that the reason many of the jobs I have delegated are done incorrectly is that I have given the instructions incorrectly.

Sometimes members of staff are timid about admitting when something is unclear, or they think they can work out a way to do it on their own. The following are guidelines I've developed from my own experience as well as from others who have learned how to delegate the hard way.

- ➢ Don't fall into the 'I can do it quicker and better' syndrome.
- ➢ Clarify the task in your own mind.
- ➢ Write an outline or sketch of what you want.
- ➢ Enlist the help of the person you're delegating to.
- ➢ Get her to write the instructions out that you give verbally.
- ➢ Don't be a perfectionist.
- ➢ Write out instructions
- ➢ Put the date and time the work is due on your requests.
- ➢ Log tasks on a job tracking sheet.
- ➢ Follow up.
- ➢ Acknowledge good jobs, no matter how small.
- ➢ Allow staff to use their own methods.

"People and organizations don't grow much without delegation and completed staff work because they are confined to the capacities of the

---

[2] Morgan, Rececca, (2015), *But I gave you instructions.*

boss and reflect both personal strengths and weaknesses." - Stephen Covey

Avoid Delegation Pitfalls

Usually discussions about avoiding pitfalls come after the process discussions. However, in this case the discussion on avoiding pitfalls is covered now because it is important to know up front what you may face in the delegation process phase.

To avoid pitfalls, you must know up front that not every task is open for delegation. Some tasks are exclusive for owner/manager and should not be delegated such as:
- Performance evaluation and feedback
- Disciplinary actions
- Politically sensitive issues
- Confrontation from interpersonal conflict

Everything else can be delegated down to the lowest organizational level that has the knowledge and skills to accept the responsibility.

The biggest pitfall to delegating is overcoming the urge of doing everything. That is a great error that prevents businesses from growing into viable companies. [3]

---

[3] Mooney, Dick, (2015)

You will know if you are digging a hole for yourself when you only talk about how much work you did and not about how much work you were able to delegate to others.

However, if you are discussing how well your employees are "stepping up" and "lightening your load," that's a good sign that you are delegating effectively. But, if you find yourself giving the following excuses to avoid delegating, you are headed in the wrong direction:

- It takes too long to explain and train.
- No one on my staff is qualified.
- I want it done right.
- My staff is already overworked.
- My employees do not want more responsibility.
- Staff may feel that the task is being imposed on them.
- Employees have not received rewards or recognitions in the past for a job well done.
- Employees may fear criticism if they don't do things exactly as expected.
- My employees cannot handle my high expectations.
- No one can do the work better than me.

- You are more comfortable doing everything yourself.
- Want to run the company only your way.
- Think that it is your job to run everything

- Others could mess up everything beyond repair
- The company is too small/young and cannot afford any mistakes
- If someone else can do my job, maybe I won't be needed anymore.
- Believe you should have full control over everything.

What it comes down to is that 'you' are the biggest barrier to delegation.

However, the more you know, understand, and practice delegation, the greater the opportunity for you to be an effective delegator. But, you must be honest with yourself in discovering the REAL reasons you don't delegate as much as you should.

Sometimes not delegating may be because you just don't know how to effectively delegate. You may have tried delegating in the past and did not have much success and decided it was not for you. If that is the case, this book should help you if you follow and practice the process.

> *"But because our organization has grown so much and in so many different ways, the delegation process places responsibility and authority on the shoulders of people you can watch grow and watch the way they treat others." - Vince McMahon*

Delegation Process

Delegation is not just one-step where you hand over a task and just hope it works out. Delegation done effectively is a process. The process consists of:

- Delegation strategies
- Assessment and analysis
- Delegate and Communicate
- Process steps
- Evaluation

The discussions in the following sections cover all the details in the delegation process.

Delegation Strategies

There are six possible delegation strategies you can take. You must choose a strategy that will match your management style and comfort level to ensure the assignment will be completed correctly. The delegation strategies are:

1. Free Rein
2. Fast Reaction Time
3. Control Right Away
4. Approval First
5. Employee Input
6. Full Control

Here are descriptions of each of the delegation strategies:

- Free Rein: "Decide the task and let the person(s) take over from there." This delegation strategy gives the most freedom. It requires a high degree of confidence in the individual abilities and decision making, as well as having good controls that will send up red flags if things get out of hand. This strategy is the ultimate delegation in giving all control to someone else.

- Fast Reaction Time: This strategy is similar to the previous one, but gives you a faster reaction time, if needed, to correct a wrong course. The confidence level in the person(s) must still be high. In this strategy, after you turn the task over to the person(s), requires them to give you their plans before starting the task(s). This strategy allows you the opportunity to correct in the very early stage of the task(s).

- Control Right Away: Make a decision on the task(s) and on who will do the task(s) then delegate and let them start planning. Then you begin to take control right away. This strategy allows you to look at the plans and the procedures before they start the task(s). This strategy saves you time, because they will do the actual planning and will do the implementation.

- Approval First: "Decide each action." The distinction between this strategy and the previous one is small but important. With this strategy, the person must get approval before proceeding on any aspect of the task(s). You may use this Strategy in instances where you do not have complete confidence in the person or the person is new. In such a case this strategy may be a useful option.

- Employee Input: In this strategy, you decide what you would do with the task(s), the options you would consider, and the pros and cons of each. Ask for the employee's analysis and recommendations. Now you are able to review the employee's thought processes while assuring yourself that their course of action will complete the task(s) correctly for the best results. This strategy is useful when the person is new and you have not worked directly with them.

- Full Control: In this strategy, you investigate the problem and the facts and decide how to handle it.   You are reserving the decision making for yourself. You control the task's decision, direction, and execution. In other words, you have full control and have given very limited delegation

It is a matter of personal preference on which delegation strategy to use. Keep in mind that there is no strategy that is better than another; it is up to what will work best for you. You may even have a blend of two or three strategies; make it work for you.

Assessment and Analysis

Once you have chosen a delegation strategy, now you are ready to conduct an assessment and analysis. The assessment and analysis phase provides you with the opportunity to plan and organize yourself before assigning the task.

The quality of your preparation determines the success of the delegation. Those who ignore planning usually keep far too much work for themselves or indiscriminately dump assignments on staff members.

During the assessment and analysis phase, you should answer the following questions:

- What should you delegate?
- What work needs to be done?
- What can and should be delegated?
- What is my best course of action, other than doing it myself, given the time constraints?
- Who should you delegate to?
- Who is the best match with the abilities and interests?
- Who would the assignment help to develop?
- Who can do it for me now?
- Who can be trained to do it?
- What is the best follow up and monitoring actions to take?
- What processes worked and what did not work?

Deciding on what you should delegate involves having a firm grasp of the duties and responsibilities of your own job. To get a good grasp of your duties and responsibilities, do the following:

- Reaffirm the primary objectives of your company/organization.
- Periodically review your duties and responsibilities.
- Highlight the "make or break" factors of your job.
- Identify those tasks that only you can do.

Delegation is normally used to give the delegator time to do things that only they can do, to improve productivity, or to develop employees. Remember, there are some tasks that you can't delegate.

As a supervisor, you must make sure you know what authorities you can entrust to your subordinates or horizontal cohorts. Never delegate tasks that require your personal authority or position to complete. Also, never delegate performance reviews, reassignment determinations, or reward/recognition decisions.

When thinking about what to delegate, it is often useful to divide your work into these time sensitive decision categories:

1. First, work that only you, the manager / supervisor, can do.
2. Second, work you can delegate as soon as someone is able to take it on.
3. Third, work that you can delegate immediately.

Once you have chosen the tasks to delegate, think about how you will track progress and how you can maintain an appropriate level of control. Develop controls that will enable you to monitor performance against the standards you desire without micro-managing the task(s).

> *"Tell me and I forget. Teach me and I remember. Involve me and I learn." - Benjamin Franklin*

Delegate and Communicate

The actual delegation starts here with assigning and communicating the assignment to the person/team. When making the delegation assignment, be sure the individual fully understands your requirements. Encourage questions, and make yourself available to answer the questions.

> *"I've learned that people will forget what you said, people will forget what you did, but people will never forget how you make them feel." - Maya Angelou*

Delegation is not just pushing work down. When you are delegating, you are consulting, developing, and assigning work. Open communication is vital, and success depends ultimately on the communication skills of the delegator and the employee, and on the quality of their relationship.

> *"To effectively communicate, we must realize that we are all different in the way we perceive the world and use this understanding as a guide to our communication with others."*
> —
>
> *Tony Robbins*

When there is a lack of trust on either side, or poor communication between them, the needed understanding and motivation are unlikely to be there. The following steps are essential in communicating an assignment:

1. Describe as fully as possible the project or task and the results expected.
2. Agree on standards of performance and timetables.
3. Determine any training or special help that will be needed and when it will be provided.
4. Define the resources available.
5. State the amount and frequency of feedback you expect.
6. Explain how much authority is being delegated.
7. Tell others who the contact person is.

Rather than rush to give "do this, do that" orders, effective delegation consists of explaining the WHAT and the WHY:

- WHAT do you want done?
- WHY did you select them to do it?
- WHAT-WHY statement should always be included.

For example:

> ➢ *I'd like you to make survey calls to find out what our customers think of our new safety product line. Given your excellent customer service skills, I believe you would represent us well in getting people talking.*
> ➢ *We need to turn in some safety reports to county regulators by next Friday, and I want you to confirm that all the numbers are up-to-date and accurate in our safety exhibits. You're a stickler for details, so I'm depending on you to crosscheck everything.*
> ➢ *Can you write a letter to our suppliers explaining our new purchasing policies? You are very familiar with our purchasing procedures and you are great at communicating. Therefore, I believe you would be very good at drafting a letter providing the information.*

To become familiar and comfortable with a WHAT-WHY statement, compose one for your next project. Don't stop there; rehearse the statement out loud to hear how it sounds.

When you've polished your WHAT-WHY statement, you're almost ready to delegate. The final step before you are ready to present the statement is to prepare answers to these three questions:

1. Who should the employee work with on this assignment? Who's available to offer help?
2. What resources or tools are available?
3. What's the deadline?

Weave the answers to the above questions into your instruction. Encourage the employee to take notes, especially to confirm the deadline so there's no misunderstanding about what you expect at that time.

> *"Take advantage of every opportunity to practice your communication skills so that when important occasions arise, you will have the gift, the style, the sharpness, the clarity, and the emotions to affect other people." - Jim Rohn*

The final step in communicating what you want done is to gauge the employee's willingness to comply. End by asking: "Do you feel comfortable tackling this?"

You might also ask for input on how the individual intends to get started.

> *"If you have an important point to make, don't try to be subtle or clever. Use a pile driver. Hit the point once. Then come back and hit it again. Then hit it a third time – tremendous whack."* – *Winston Churchill*

Initially, delegation can feel more like a hassle than it's worth. However, by delegating effectively, you can expand the amount of work you can deliver.

When you arrange the workload so that you are working on the tasks that have the highest priority for you, and other people are working on meaningful and challenging assignments, you have a recipe for success.

Process Steps

Now that you are familiar and understand the overall delegation process, this section will expand in depth using a 9-step delegation process. The delegation steps are:

1. Determine what to delegate
2. Select the right person
3. Delegate the assignment
4. Describe the responsibilities
5. Ask questions, make suggestions, get commitment

6. Listen carefully to comments and respond accordingly and be encouraging
7. Establish process to monitor progress
8. Allow for creativity and varied work styles
9. Recognize and reward

The following are descriptions of each of the steps in the delegation process. To be effective in the delegation process, it is very important for you to complete each of the 9-steps.

Do not take short cuts because you will run the risk of miscommunication and receiving the wrong outcome from the task.

1. Determine what to delegate

Determine what you are going to delegate. Then take the time to plan how you are going to present the assignment, including your requirements, parameters, authority level, checkpoints and expectations.

Define the scope of the work based on the outcomes, products, and deliverables. Break out the tasks or steps that will accomplish the work.

Decide on project milestones and define realistic completion dates for each one. Then delineate the steps for each task and decide on the skill sets needed.

As a safe guard, write down these items and give a copy to your delegatee. The will appreciate having a written point of reference.

> *"Words, once they are printed, have a life of their own." - Carol Burnett*

2. Select the right person

Assess the skills and the experience of your employees as objectively as possible. Don't be too quick to choose the person who you always know you can depend on.

Next, identify the people for each task. Look for dependability and motivation as well as skill. The way you present a task can bolster someone's willingness to participate, or to stretch beyond their comfort zone, and follow through.

When you delegate a new job to someone, convey enthusiasm and emphasize the importance of the project in a positive manner. Describe the task to people in ways that appeal to their needs and values.

People are motivated when an assignment matches their talents, needs, and skills. You compliment people when you ask them to take on a task that matches or expands their skills. People enjoy showing off what they know.

To make the match, get to know people. Find out about their experience, education, hobbies, and training. If you are organizing a team or committee, make sure the members have a good mix of talents and strengths.

Some people work well with little supervision, while some expect routine guidance. Some like working with technical details, while others like working with global concepts. Some excel in the limelight, while some work well behind the scenes. Structure your group with diversity and balance.

The person assigned the task can feel more empowered being assigned the entire job rather than only a fragment of a project.

If a job is too large to assign to one person, create a team with a lead team member. Then the team can be rewarded for a job well done.

3. Delegate the assignment

Give an overview of the assignment including the importance of the assignment and why you have chosen the employee for the job.

Very important to include in delegating the assignment is to define the desired outcome and let the person complete the task in the manner they choose as long as the results are as you have specified.

Provide enough information - One of the most common reasons delegation fails is that the leader does not take the time and energy necessary to provide complete information team members need to guide their performance.

Stand ready to help but don't take the job back. A leader must stand by to help team members over the rough spots, especially when the leader has knowledge and experience doing the job and when the team member asks for help. But the leader must do everything possible to avoid taking the job back.

Keep in mind, if you're not willing to live with a few mistakes here and there, your team members will never develop the experience and skill to stand on their own.

Break up big jobs - The key to delegating large, complex jobs or jobs that have never been done before is to delegate gradually.

First assign a small task leading to a little progress and then add another small task which builds upon the first. When that is achieved, add another stage; and so on.

4. Describe the responsibilities

Clearly communicate to each team member the purpose of the project, his or her responsibilities and schedule. Specify and quantify what you expect for the final outcome and/or interim products. <u>Example:</u> "We need 1000 copies of a five-page report by December 5." Give people outlines, checklists, and diagrams.

Explain how each task dovetails with, or supports, or is contingent on other tasks. Provide access to or direct people to relevant reference materials such as training manuals, users' guides, and workbooks.

In detail, outline sub-tasks, defining any necessary parameters, and setting performance standards. Make sure the employee understands his/her level or degree of authority.

Let the employee know who they can turn to for help as well as other available resources. Be sure to notify those affected by the delegatee's power.

Maintain management control but don't nag. Management control is simply defined as comparing what is with what and should take corrective action when the two are not in sync.

The best way to avoid Micromanaging is for the leader and team member to agree on up front when it is a good time for the team member to report on progress.

5. Ask questions and make suggestions, get commitment

Ask questions to make sure they understand the task. Give every person your contact information and make yourself available to answer questions and provide guidance and clarification.

Offer the employee help or some type of back-up assistance. An employee who already feels overwhelmed may worry about completing the assignments already on their plate.

It is your responsibility to help establish priorities and relieve some of the pressure by getting someone else to share some of the delegatee's routine tasks for the duration of the assignment.

6. Listen carefully to comments and respond accordingly and be encouraging

This step helps to get employee "buy-in" and will also help you determine if the employee does indeed understand what is expected.

Express confidence in the employee's ability to successfully handle the new responsibility. Be encouraging.

> *"Words of comfort, skillfully administered, are the oldest therapy known to man."* Louis Nizer

7. Establish a process to monitor progress

Establish checkpoints, deadlines, and ways to monitor progress. The entire discussion should be a collaborative process. You should strive for mutual agreement among the team.

Check in periodically and ask your team about their progress. Ask questions such as:
- Are they on schedule?
- Do they have the resources they need?
- Have they run up against any unforeseen obstacles?
- Do they still understand the requirements?
- How are they coming along on the layout?
- What are they working on now?
- What have they accomplished since we last talked?

Monitor the work and give feedback in a positive, helpful way. Provide sincere praise and positive reinforcement for all efforts.

If the work is behind schedule, or the finished products are flawed, maintain a helpful, open attitude. Explore with team members how improvements could be made. Ask what additional help or resources they need. Help them brainstorm new strategies.

You may want to restructure work assignments, or assign a mentor to an employee who isn't learning quickly. You may need to bring in a specialist or negotiate with the customer for a later delivery date.

Observe the checkpoints you and the employee agreed on.

> *"My belief is that communication is the best way to create strong relationships." -*
> *Jada Pinkett Smith*

8. Allow for creativity and varied work styles

Keep your focus on the final result/products, not on the details of how the job gets done. People work according to individual learning styles and preferences. When you let them work in their preferred ways, they feel ownership for the effort.

While some people like to work piece-meal, some like to work through continuous effort. Some people can multi-task, and some like to work on one thing at a time. Some need more structure and supervision than others.

Those on your team may not perform the task exactly as you would. However, if you have selected skilled, talented people, they will probably do the job better than you would have and you may be pleasantly surprised with the results.

9. Recognize and reward

Always recognize and reward the person for their successful completion of the assignment as well as at the checkpoints and deadlines.

Provide incentives and show appreciation. Let people know there is a pay-off in working for you, and develop a reputation as someone who rewards good work. Pay increases, bonuses, stock options, and promotions are significant incentives for getting people to go the extra mile.

You can give other rewards too, such as time off, a letter of appreciation in the personnel file, special mention in the corporate or industry newsletter, an award, a gift, or an invitation to a special corporate/industry event for insiders only.

Evaluate and reward good performance - Leaders should constantly evaluate the performance of team members on delegated tasks. Make suggestions, and provide support when necessary, and give both private and public praise when jobs are done well.

Because delegating frees time for developing the 'big picture', for business owners, executive team members, managers, and supervisors, there is no more important activity than delegation. As a manager, it is your job to get work done in collaboration with others.

"I'm a great believer that any tool that enhances communication has profound effects in terms of how people can learn from each other, and how they can achieve the kind of freedoms that they're interested in." - Bill Gates

To be able to recognize and reward your staff for the progress and 'jobs well done', it is helpful to assess the progress of their work. The following are some techniques to track employee's work progress:

1. Scrutinize and approve every step of the assignment before the worker proceeds to the next stage.

   You ensure the project is completed satisfactorily, and you can satisfy your urge to know what's going on throughout the process.

   However, the down side is that you might make the employee feel stupid by signing off on each step. You risk showing you don't trust others to think for themselves without your constant oversight. Plus, it takes up more of your time.

2. Set a date for the individual to complete the work. Instruct the employee to come to you with any questions along the way; otherwise, you stay out of it.

This technique gives the worker a chance to operate independently without lots of interference. Your hands-off role also frees you to do what's most important.

However, the down side is that you may have no way of knowing how its going unless the employee chooses to keep you informed.

3. Designate a manager who's in charge of overseeing the employee's work. This is really double delegation: you're assigning work to someone and assigning a supervisor to monitor that work.

   With this technique, you increase the odds the work will get done properly — without having to spend time tracking it yourself.

   However with this technique, In a fast-growing business, you may not have the luxury of putting a manager in charge of monitoring an employee's work.

> *"Nothing is impossible; the word itself says 'I'm possible!"* - *Audrey Hepburn*

Delegation Evaluation

Delegation doesn't end after the assignment. Following up, monitoring performance, providing support and feedback are crucial steps of the process. Evaluating the task ensures that the task is completed on time and accurately.

In your assignment of tasks, you should have outlined or scheduled regular progress reports to allow you to monitor the assignment and answer any questions that may have arisen. This process allows you to keep track of progress but also allows the employee to complete the assignment in his/her own manner and observe the deadlines and checkpoints for themselves.

Evaluation Tips:
- Reiterate your support, remind the employee of the resources available.
- Provide both positive and corrective feedback so the employee has an opportunity to make necessary changes before the deadline. Remember, the ultimate responsibility for the task is still in your hands.
- Clarify roles, authority, objectives periodically to check understanding of the delegated task. Don't forget that delegation is part of skill development so add some time for debriefing upon completion of the assignment.

- Discuss what worked, what did not work so well, and what you would do differently next time.

Brief your team member appropriately. Take time to explain why they were chosen for the job, what's expected from them during the project, the goals you have for the project, all timelines and deadlines and the resources on which they can draw. Agree a schedule for checking-in with progress updates.

Finally, make sure that the team member knows that you want to know if any problems occur, and that you are available for any questions or guidance needed as the work progresses.

> *"You have no power at all if you do not exercise constant power." – Major Owens*

In delegating effectively, we have to find the sometimes-difficult balance between giving enough space for people to use their abilities to best effect, while still monitoring and supporting closely enough to ensure that the job is done correctly and effectively.

Full Acceptance Evaluation

When delegated work is delivered back to you, be sure to set aside time to review the work thoroughly.

Only accept good quality, fully-complete work. If you accept work you are not satisfied with, your team member does not learn to do the job properly. Worse than this, you accept a whole new precedent of work that you will probably need to complete yourself. Not only does this overload you, it means that you don't have the time to do your own job properly.

Of course, when good work is returned to you, make sure to both recognize and reward the effort.

As a leader, you should get in the practice of complimenting members of your team every time you are impressed with what they have done. The effort on your part will go a long way toward building team member's self-confidence and efficiency, both of which will be improved on the next delegated task; hence, you both win.

> *"It's never what you say, but how you make it sound sincere." - Marya Mannes*

Chapter V

Exercises and Activities to
Sharpen Your Delegation Skills

A great deal of information has been covered in this book. In mastering the art of delegation, you will want to test your knowledge and skill on the topic. In this Chapter you have an opportunity to test your knowledge on how to effectively delegate.

Test yourself and review the information in the book and then re-test until you are at a comfort level to execute what you have learned.

The best teacher and evaluator is experience. The more you put into practice what you have learned about delegation, the better you will perform in the art.

The following pages contain exercises and activities for you to complete to test and sharpen your delegation skills.

Activity 1:

How Well Do You Delegate?[4]

This activity will help identify your strengths and determine where improvement would be beneficial. Circle the number that best describes you and then total the numbers and rate your skills. The higher the number, the more the statement matches your skills.

5 = always
4 = most of the time
3 = sometimes
2 = weak in this area
1 = rarely

1. Each of my subordinates know what I expect of him
5 4 3 2 1

2. I involve employees in goal setting, problem solving and productivity-improvement activities   5 4 3 2 1

3. I place my personal emphasis on planning, organizing, motivating and controlling rather than on doing tasks others could do   5 4 3 2 1

4. When assigning tasks, I select the assignee thoughtfully
5 4 3 2 1

5. When a problem occurs on a project I have delegated, I give the employee a reasonable chance to work it out for themselves   5 4 3 2 1

---

[4] How to Delegate Effectively, *DirJournal Guides, How to Guides - Small Business Guides,* Tuesday, March 3, 2009.

6. When I delegate work to employees, I brief them fully on the details of the assignment   5 4 3 2 1

7. I see delegation as one way to help employees develop their knowledge, skills and expertise   5 4 3 2 1

8. When I delegate a project, I make sure that everyone involved knows who is in charge   5 4 3 2 1

9. When delegating a task, I balance authority with need and experience   5 4 3 2 1

10. I hold my employees responsible for results 5 4 3 2 1

A score between 41 and 50 indicates you are on target. A score between 31 and 40 indicates you are getting and need improvement. Scores below 40 indicates you need to make immediate changes in your delegation skills.

Activity 2:

Do you Really Delegate?[5]
Test Your Delegation Skills

To find out of you actually delegate, answer each of the
statements below using the following codes:

1 = always

2 = sometimes

3 = never

_____ I find that my employees consistently look for
ways to relieve the pressure that top management
faces — without being asked.

_____ I'm free to "think big" because my colleagues and
employees handle all the daily operational stuff.

_____ As my company continues to grow rapidly, I'm
totally comfortable letting go and putting others
in charge of pieces of my business — rather than
clinging to control.

_____ I prefer to spend 30 minutes training an employee
to do a new task than just doing it myself in five
minutes.

_____ I say to an employee "Let me show you how to do

---

[5] How to Delegate Effectively, *An Edward Lowe In-depth Business Builder,* Lawson Consulting Group Inc., 2008.

that" far more than I think to myself "If I don't do it, it won't get done right."

_____ I look for opportunities to praise my managers for delegating to their workers.

Review your answers. If your total score is 6-8, then you're an excellent delegator. All you need is reinforcement of your delegation skills.

If your score is 9-14, you're on the road to becoming an effective delegator. You need a little more awareness and effort to coach others to plug the holes and take more responsibility.

For those who score over 14, you're not alone. Many entrepreneurs need to confront the fact that they just can't do it all, and that assigning jobs to others is a vital part of building a business. Work on connecting the drive, skills, and talents of *every employee,* and delegate.

Activity 3:

Delegation Practice With Your Current Tasks

This activity is designed to give you practice in selecting what to delegate by using the current task you are working on. Completing this activity will help you decide which tasks you will delegate from your current work.

Follow the instructions given below.
1. Make a list of specific tasks that you can currently working on.
2. Select one of the tasks from your list
3. Answer the following questions for the task:

- What work needs to be done?
- What can and should be delegated?
- What is the best match of work with the employees' abilities and interests?
- Who would the assignment help to develop?
- Who can do it for me now?
- Who can be trained to do it?
- What is the best course of action, other than doing it myself, given the time constraints involved?
4. Delegate to employees who are eager and interested in their own jobs and who want to expand their roles.

Tips

Enthusiastic, high performing employees who need additional challenges are excellent candidates for delegation. However, don't avoid employees who have failed in delegated tasks in the past if they have learned from their experience or have received additional training.

Keep in mind that some of the best learned lessons come from times we did not succeed.

Delegation is an important tool for assessing potential, training, and development. You should direct delegated tasks to employees who can benefit the most.

Try to avoid delegating the same task to the same employee every time. Spread delegated tasks around to get a look at the capabilities of many employees and to train the maximum number of them for new assignments.

ACTIVITY 4:

TO WHOM SHOULD YOU DELEGATE?[6]

Choose a task you want to delegate and decide who on your staff would be the appropriate person to receive the task.

Effective delegation requires effective communication. Communicate and assign the task in an organized, thoughtful and thorough manner by doing the following:

- State a clear objective.
- Determine guidelines for the assignment.
- Set necessary limitations or constraints.
- Grant the person the authority to carry out the assignment.
- Set a deadline for completion of the assignment.
- Decide the best means for the employee to provide you with regular progress reports.

To delegate effectively, the employee must have both the responsibility and the accountability for

---

[6] Office of Human Resource Management | Louisiana State University *Management in State Government Participant's Manual)*

completing the assignment. The delegation process will not be successful without you granting clearly, the authority to make necessary decisions and to take action to complete the assignment. This step is particularly important if your employee is working with others and will need to gather information, resources, or materials.

Activity 5

Symptoms of Poor Delegation

There are many symptoms of poor delegation that can be seen in the working habits of the manager, the attitude of the employees, or the overall productivity in the organization.

Place a checkmark on the following list of symptoms that are visible in your department / organization:

1. Deadlines are frequently missed
2. Some employees are much busier than others
3. Competent employees feel frustrated and bored
4. Manager is usually too busy to talk to employees
5. Employees are assigned the tasks without proper training
6. Employees are unsure of their authority and responsibility
7. Employees' suggestions are often neglected and overlooked
8. Employees frequently request transfers to other departments
9. Manager never has time to visit the employees' work stations
10. Changes in plans and objectives are not passed on to employees
11. Communication flow is very slow, incomplete and often too late

12. The department/organization is plagued by slow decision making
13. Manager sometimes intervenes in the task without informing subordinates
14. Manager insists that all incoming/outgoing mail must first pass through them
15. Manager does not meet the deadline
16. Manager often takes the office work home
17. Manager sometimes delays / postpones vacation because of the work load

If you have checked one or two of the above statements, you should look very carefully at your delegation practices. Ask yourself why these conditions exist in your department / organization.

References

Lueke, Richard & McIntosh, Perry. (2009) The Busy Manager's Guide to Delegation. American Management Association.

Maddux, R. B. (1997). Get Results with Delegation. Secretary. Vol. 57 (1).

Masak, I. (1992). Dare to Delegate. CMA Magazine. Vol. 66 (8).

Mooney, Dick, (2015)

Morgan, Rececca, (2015), *But I gave you instructions.*

Painter, C. (1995). Effective Delegation for the New Supervisor. Supervision. Vol. 56 (8).

Pollar, O. & Solmo, R. (1996). Giving Up Control. Successful Meetings. Vol. 45 (1).

Swinton, Lyndsay. (2014), Management for the Rest of Us, www.mftrou.com.

How to Delegate Effectively, *DirJournal Guides, How to Guides - Small Business Guides,* Tuesday, March 3, 2009.

How to Delegate Effectively, *An Edward Lowe In-depth Business Builder,* Lawson Consulting Group Inc., 2008.

Office of Human Resource Management, Louisiana State University, Baton Rouge LA 70803, *Management in State Government Participant's Manual*, 2015

www.ingramcontent.com/pod-product-compliance
Lightning Source LLC
Chambersburg PA
CBHW060638210326
41520CB00010B/1648